Happy
Houseplants

Happy
Houseplants

grow your own indoor oasis

CICO BOOKS
LONDON NEW YORK

Stylist Marisa Daly
Designer Geoff Borin
Editor Sophie Devlin
Picture research Jess Walton
Production manager Gordana Simakovic
Senior commissioning editor Annabel Morgan
Art director Sally Powell
Creative director Leslie Harrington

Some of the text and images in this book first appeared in *The House Gardener*,
published in 2014, and *House Plants*, published in 2016.

For photography and artwork credits and copyright information,
see page 144.

Published in 2024 by CICO Books, an imprint of Ryland Peters & Small Ltd
20–21 Jockey's Fields   341 E 116th St
London WC1R 4BW   New York, NY 10029

www.rylandpeters.com

10 9 8 7 6 5 4 3 2 1

A CIP catalog record for this book is available from the Library of Congress
and the British Library.

ISBN 978-1-80065-311-5

Printed in China

Contents

Introduction

Living in the city, I am very aware that outdoor space is at a premium. During the winter, while looking out at my balconies and dreaming of the summer, I started thinking: what if you wanted to have that little bit of green, but didn't have any outside space at all? This turned my attention indoors, where I have noticed a renewed interest in houseplants. Even if you live in the country, indoor plants can offer some much-needed contact with nature, something that is very important, not only in terms of aesthetics, but also to promote a healthy emotional environment. Houseplants bring their natural form, color, and fragrance to the home, and can add the finishing touch to an interior scheme.

Historically, plants have been used indoors for centuries—indeed, medieval paintings depict Crusaders returning with plant specimens from many corners of the world. The nineteenth century was a golden age of plant collecting, which went hand in hand with the Victorians' passion for exploration and discovery. The legacy of these adventurous plant explorers lives on in the plants that thrive in our modern natural landscape and in our homes.

In this book, I will show you how to choose, grow, and decorate with houseplants, as well as guide you through the different techniques needed to care for your new "green guests" and keep your houseplants happy.

The
essentials

Top 10 Houseplant Tips

Position plants carefully

Choose plants that suit the environment, since even the most dedicated gardener can't make a sun-loving plant thrive in a cold, shady area. So, ensure that your plants are suited to the light levels and temperature of the room in which they will be living.

2

Try to avoid direct sun

Windowsills in direct sunlight will be too
hot for most houseplants. Similarly, try
not to place your plants over a direct
source of heat, such as a radiator.

3

Avoid shady areas

At the same time, you need to ensure there is sufficient
light for your houseplants to photosynthesize effectively.

4

Avoid temperature extremes

Keep delicate plants away from drafts, since
these will decrease humidity levels.

Pot on regularly

Aim to repot your houseplants into larger
pots every two years or so. This will ensure
that they are not stressed and will thrive.

6

Be well equipped

Use the proper tools for indoor gardening.
A long-spouted watering can and a mister to increase
humidity are both essential for reducing dust levels,
as well as dealing with pest and disease outbreaks.
A long-handled fork and a pair of scissors are great for
accessing difficult areas, while a sponge attached
to a long handle will keep glass containers clean.

7

Water wisely

Don't overwater houseplants; adding some drainage material at the bottom of the pot will help to keep roots aerated and ensure that they don't drown.

8

Give your plants a break

Allow houseplants to rest during the winter period and move them to a cooler position. This is because most plants are dormant at this time, and so don't need as much sunlight. You should also reduce the amount of water and food you provide, as this can help to prevent diseases such as mold and root rot. Move plants away from windows, because these areas will be too cold in the winter.

9

Be vigilant

Learn to recognize potential problems early on, before a pest infestation or other physiological problem kills off your plant. For example, danger signs for low air humidity include buds falling off, leaves withering, and leaves with brown tips. Signs of high humidity include mold, rot, and soft growth. See pages 128–141 for more information.

10

Think long-term

Some popular houseplant gifts only have a short growing period, so choose plants that will thrive for longer if you want a year-round display.

Light levels and photosynthesis

The process of photosynthesis provides plants with energy and occurs naturally as a result of the green pigment chlorophyll in their leaves and stems. Sunlight acts on the chlorophyll to produce carbohydrates such as glucose, using carbon dioxide from the air and water from the soil. Oxygen and water vapor are released into the air as by-products of the process, which is why plants are so beneficial to us indoors.

Most houseplants, including orchids (opposite) and bromeliads, thrive in filtered sunlight, but all green-leaved plants such as philodendrons can live happily away from windows and even in the shade. However, plants with variegated or colored leaves, flowering plants, and cacti and succulents must have good light levels to flower and flourish in your home.

Temperature and humidity

Every plant has a preferred temperature range in which it will grow well, and it will die if exposed to temperatures outside this range for a long period of time. You should also avoid extreme fluctuations in temperature, as this will shock the plant. As a guide, bear the following ideal temperatures in mind:

- The minimum winter temperature (and for winter dormancy) is 55°F (12°C).

- The average temperature for plants to thrive is 65–75°F (18–24°C).

- Plants from less tropical regions grow well in 50–60°F (10–16°C).

- Fluctuations of 20°F (11°C) or more within 24 hours are detrimental to all plants, so keep temperatures constant.

- Young seedlings will grow best in a constant temperature.

It is also advisable to match the humidity levels to the plant; for example, cacti need a dry atmosphere. If you wish to raise the humidity, try grouping plants together in one place and misting them regularly.

Potting mixes

Most indoor plants will thrive in sterile, soil-less potting mix (made with a peat substitute). It is not recommended that you use soil from your garden, as this may contain fungi, weeds, pests, soil-borne diseases, seeds, or toxins that can prevent your plants from growing well.

Specialty potting mixes are also available for particular plants with specific needs, including ericaceous potting mix for lime-hating plants, such as camellias, and gritty, fast-draining potting mix for cacti. Coarse, low-nutrient potting mixes, which contain vermiculite and perlite, are ideal for orchids because they need good drainage. This is because orchids are particularly sensitive and don't like getting their roots wet. You can use a seedling potting mix for sowing seeds and growing seedlings.

Decorative toppings

Using a decorative topping not only finishes off your container aesthetically, but also helps the plant to retain moisture. You will need to move the decorative topping aside slightly when checking if your plant needs watering. I have listed my favorites below, but again, it's a case of personal choice—just remember to match the topping to your container and its surroundings.

MOSS is ideal for top-dressing container plantings and there are many different varieties to choose from. Reindeer moss is wonderful used in combination with sand toppings. Sphagnum moss is perfect for covering the potting mix in terrariums. Fern or sheet moss makes a great cover for large-scale planters owing to its size. Pillow moss—often known as clump or cushion moss—forms neat clumps, which range from small, round mounds to larger, irregular shapes. Pillow moss is great for making miniature gardens.

SAND looks lovely on simple story gardens and is particularly nice to use when you're planting up a container as a project with children. Aquatic sands give a finer finish and are available in many colors.

PEBBLES are available in various shapes, sizes, and finishes from garden and aquatic centers.

WOODCHIPS are perfect for arrangements that have a more natural, earthy feel.

FINE GRAVEL is great for giving a more organic feel to your planting display.

SHELLS can be great fun to find on trips to the beach.

SLATE CHIPS work well with sleek, modern arrangements.

Selecting a healthy plant

When buying a houseplant from a garden center or nursery, take the time to check that you have chosen a healthy specimen that will thrive once you get home. The following checklist should help you to make a good choice:

- Look for strong, healthy leaves with a good, vibrant color.
  Avoid any plant with damaged or blotchy leaves.

- The plant's stems should be firm and, if the plant is flowering, choose one that has lots of unopened buds for a longer flowering period.

- Check that there is no space between the potting mix and the inside of the pot, because this means the plant is extremely dry and will grow poorly.

- Make sure there are no insects or larvae on the plant;
  you don't want to introduce pest infestations into your home.

- Avoid diseased plants with furry mold or any unsightly blotches.

- Check for any curled or withered leaves, which indicate
  that the plant won't grow well in future.

- Check that there are no soggy, wilted patches, since this
  suggests that the plant has root rot or is pot-bound.

- Check that the roots are not growing out of the bottom of the pot. This means that the plant is pot-bound and so has been under stress.

- Buy a younger plant if possible because, although it will be smaller, it will adapt to its new environment better.

- When taking your plant home, make sure it is wrapped properly, to ensure that there is no damage to the leaves during transit.

- Don't place the plant in direct sunlight for the first few weeks, so that it can acclimatize before you move it to its final position. However, if you are buying a flowering plant, place it in its final sunny position immediately.

Planting a container

There will be times when you need to pot up a plant, especially if you purchase it in an ugly plastic container. You may also need to repot a plant in order to give it a new lease of life or when it has outgrown its container.

1

Cover the bottom of the container with a layer of drainage material, such as gravel or pebbles, aiming to fill about a quarter of the container's volume. This will allow the roots to breathe and prevent them from drowning.

2

Fill the container with potting mix to bring the plant up so that the top of the root-ball is just beneath the rim of the container. Try to position the plant centrally in the container and make sure it is not lopsided.

3

Carefully feed more potting mix in between the plant and container, and firm it down. Avoid compacting the potting mix too much, though, as this will hinder drainage.

4

Add a layer of decorative mulch, such as fine gravel or shells, to finish off the planting (see page 28). Not only does this make the container look more attractive, but it can also help to reduce the rate of evaporation.

How to water

You should water plants more in spring and summer when they are actively growing and less when they are resting in winter. You can check whether a plant needs to be watered by pushing your fingers into the surface of the potting mix to a depth of about ½in (1cm). If the mix is not moist, then the plant needs to be watered. If there is a decorative topping in the container, scrape a little away to reach the potting mix.

There are two ways to water. You can water from above, which is the most convenient method and ensures an even distribution of water. Make sure there is a lip of about 1–1½in (2–3cm) between the potting mix and the top of the pot. This will allow the maximum amount of water to reach the plant. Alternatively, you can water from below, which involves watering the saucer to avoid wetting the crown of the plant and causing it to rot. This is particularly useful for fleshy plants such as cyclamen.

Vacation watering

One of the most common ways to kill a plant is by underwatering it, which can be a problem when you are away. Use these techniques to protect your plants.

CAPILLARY MATTING: This is available from garden centers (I usually find that 3ft/1m is sufficient). Fill the sink three-quarters full with water and dunk the capillary matting so that it is evenly moist. Put one end of the matting in the water and drape the other end over the draining board, then place the pots on the matting. This won't work on plants with drainage material in the bottom of their containers, as the potting mix has to be in contact with the matting.

WICK SYSTEM: This method (opposite) uses a long, narrow piece of capillary matting. Position a bowl so that it is higher than the level of the potting mix. Fill the bowl with water and put the piece of matting in the water, weighing it down with a stone. Push the other end of the matting into the potting mix.

SLOW-SEEPAGE SYSTEM: Take a cut-off water bottle with the lid end intact. Bore a few holes in the lid to allow the water to drain through slowly. Push the lid end into the potting mix and fill the bottle with water.

Increasing humidity

There are a number of ways to increase the level of humidity around plants, such as misting the leaves with a spray bottle (below). You can also stand a plant in a tray or saucer and spread a layer of pebbles around it. Fill the saucer with water so that the moist pebbles increase the humidity. Air plants (opposite) need regular misting because they take their moisture in from the air.

Feeding

Feeding indoor plants is essential if they are to remain healthy. There are three major constituents of plant food: nitrogen (N) for leaf growth and "greening" up yellowing plants; phosphorous (P) for root growth; and potassium (K) for flowers. Remember to look at the ingredients before you buy.

Feeding is generally carried out only during the growing season, when watering frequency is high. If you have just repotted your plant, you have a couple of months before the food in the potting mix runs out. Most plants benefit from a feed every two to four weeks using one of these methods.

POWDER AND LIQUID FEEDS: These are diluted with water and applied at regular intervals. A balanced liquid feed will meet the needs of most plants, but there are also specialty formulas available for orchids and citrus plants.

FERTILIZER GRANULES: These are added to the potting mix when you plant up the container.

FERTILIZER STICKS: These are simply pushed into the potting mix to provide a slowly released supply of nutrients.

Potting on

Container plants eventually outgrow their pots, and these cramped conditions can result in a pot-bound plant. This is where the root system has wrapped itself around the pot, creating an impenetrable wall. As a result, the plant cannot access sufficient water or nutrients. The term "potting on" means potting a plant into a larger container where it will have ample room to grow. The steps for potting on are the same as for planting a new container (see page 33).

Pruning

The main reasons for pruning are what are often referred to as "the three Ds": removing dead, damaged, or diseased stems. Bushy plants will need their growing points and side branches pruned to maintain their structure. Pruning can be done at any time, but the best time is in spring, when new growth is more vigorous. Here are a few helpful pruning techniques to get you started.

MAKING PRUNING CUTS: You can either make a slanted cut just above an outward-facing bud or make a straight cut across the stem above a pair of opposite buds. You don't want to damage the bud, but making a cut too far away from it may promote disease in the stem.

PINCHING OUT: Natural growth hormones are found in the highest concentrations in the growing tips of the plant. If you remove the growing tips, the hormones in the other parts of the plant will be triggered into producing side shoots. To promote dense, bushy growth, pinch out growing tips on climbing plants using your finger and thumb. Hand pruners (secateurs) can be used on plants that have tougher stems.

DEADHEADING: Plants usually stop growing once they have set seed, so removing spent flowers encourages new buds to develop. Removing tired flowers will also reduce the risk of petals falling onto leaves and causing rot. When deadheading, try to cut off as much of the flower as possible.

Cacti and succulents

The word "succulent" is a descriptive term given to those plants that store water in their leaves or stems. Cacti belong to a large family of plants that are all succulents. There are also other types of succulent besides cacti. So, as a rule, remember that all cacti are succulents, but not all succulents are cacti. Succulents are found in many countries all over the world and have always held an attraction for gardeners because of their exotic appearance.

During the 15th century, Portuguese explorers collected succulents such as *Aloe*, *Haworthia* and *Stapelia* from Africa and *Caralluma* and *Euphorbia* (spurge) from India. The Dutch East India Company, which was established in 1602, was also responsible for collecting many succulent species for the Dutch government. Many of these succulents also found their way to the world-famous Royal Botanic Gardens at Kew, in London.

Desert cacti and succulents like a warm, sunny location where they will receive around four to six hours of warm sunlight every day. Place cacti in the sunniest spot in your home, perhaps on a windowsill or a table close to a window. Please note that forest cacti, such as *Schlumbergera* (Christmas cactus), will need some shade and less intense heat than desert cacti in summer, as well as a potting mix rich in organic matter and a little humidity.

POTTING MIX: Use a potting mix specially formulated for cacti and succulents with added gravel and sand.

WATERING: Water cacti and succulents as needed—about once a month. A good indication that your cacti need watering is to lift the pot and see how heavy it is. If the pot feels lighter than usual, it's time to water your plant.

FEEDING: Feed cacti with a houseplant fertilizer that is high in nitrates and phosphorus. Feed once or twice a year, diluting the fertilizer to half the manufacturer's recommended amount.

HANDLING CACTI: Always use a strip of newspaper or card when handling cacti to avoid pricking your fingers.

Useful tools

The tools and materials you use are really important when caring for and maintaining your houseplants. You don't need to spend a fortune, however, as many tools can be made from household items. Here, I have outlined the most useful tools for all the projects in this book.

MINI SPADES OR TROWELS for digging holes and moving objects in containers.

MINI RAKE for raking over and patting down the potting mix.

STICKS are great for moving and positioning plants in difficult areas and also for making holes in the potting mix when you are sowing seeds.

STIFF PAPER for making a funnel to pour materials into small, difficult-to-access containers.

LONG-HANDLED TWEEZERS are useful for grabbing plants when you're positioning them in small containers.

A MAGNIFYING GLASS is helpful for enlarging small objects when planting up a terrarium.

SCISSORS are one of the most useful tools, as you will find them really helpful for deadheading, trimming back, tidying up, pruning, and taking cuttings.

LONG-HANDLED SCISSORS are great for pruning and tweaking off dead leaves.

LEAF PRUNERS are really useful for cutting more woody and mature plant stems that cannot be cut with a pair of scissors.

ROOT CLIPPERS are a great tool when you're repotting plants (especially bonsai) and also for propagating plants by division.

HOMEMADE GLASS CLEANER for cleaning difficult-to-reach areas inside pots, glass vases, and terrariums. To make your own, simply stick a small sponge onto the end of a chopstick.

SMALL BRUSHES are useful for brushing stray potting mix from leaves.

BAMBOO STICKS AND TRELLIS are ideal for providing plants such as climbers with a form of support, and for training plants.

WIRE for training plants, such as *Passiflora* (passionflower) and *Hedera* (ivy), as well as for tying in untidy branches. A good green-coated floristry wire is perfect, as the green will blend in with the plant.

FLORISTRY PINS are great for holding down mosses and fixing parts of clump moss together.

A BALL OF STRING is useful for securing climbing plants and fixing moss around plants, such as in the hanging fruit garden project.

PLANT LABELS are helpful when sowing different seeds, so that you can remember what they are.

SPRAY BOTTLES can be used for misting plants, as well as for treating pests with pesticides or fungicides.

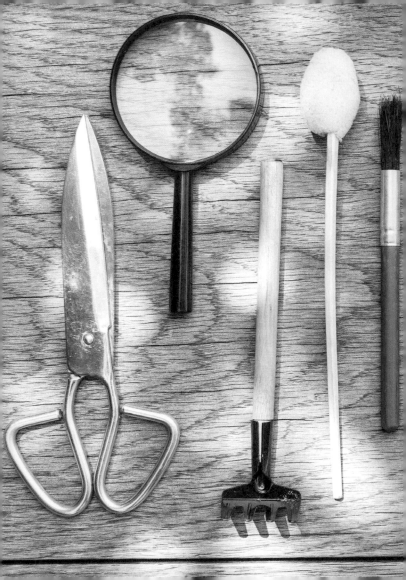

An A to Z
of amazing
plants

Achimenes species

The flowers of these plants appear on short stems
that grow from the leaf axils.

SITE: Keep out of direct sunlight.

TEMPERATURE: Average room temperature (65–75°F/
18–24°C). Achimenes will tolerate temperatures as low as
55°F (12°C), but anything above 80°F (25°C) will cause
the flower buds to shrivel and dry up.

WATERING: Keep the potting mix evenly moist at all times. If
the growing medium is allowed to dry out, the plant will
become dormant. Do not water in winter.

FEEDING: Feed fortnightly while the plant is blooming with a
high-phosphorous liquid fertilizer diluted to a quarter strength.

TIP: Achimenes will go dormant in winter. When flowering
tapers off in the fall (autumn), reduce watering and allow
the plant to die back naturally.

Adiantum species
(Maidenhair fern)

Maidenhair ferns are foliage plants with arching, black, wiry fronds covered with triangular green leaflets called pinnae.

SITE: Moderate to bright light. No direct sun.

TEMPERATURE: Average room temperature (60–75°F/16–24°C).

WATERING: Do not allow the roots of these ferns to become too wet or to dry out.

FEEDING: Feed once a month from spring through summer with a liquid fertilizer diluted to half strength.

TIP: This tropical native demands high levels of humidity that are not practical in most homes. For this reason, these plants are best grown in terrariums where humidity is naturally high.

"All gardeners live in beautiful places because they make them so."

—Joseph Joubert

I HAVE PLANTS

THIS WEEKEND

Aloe vera

Thriving without the need for much care, this plant is an ideal choice for busy or absent-minded plant-lovers.

SITE: Aloes will thrive in sun, but may turn brown in harsh light. Indirect sunlight is best.

TEMPERATURE: Average room temperature (65–75°F/18–24°C).

WATERING: Avoid overwatering, because this is a succulent. Allow the potting mix to become fairly dry before you water again. Water lightly during the winter months as the potting mix will dry out more slowly.

FEEDING: Feed at about a quarter of the usual dilution once a month over the growing season.

TIP: The gel found inside this plant is cooling and soothing for all sorts of skin problems, including burns, cuts, stings, bruises, and rashes, as well as for welts, itching, blisters, infections, and abrasions.

Aphelandra squarrosa

(Zebra plant)

This plant is highly recommended for its dramatic foliage and beautiful bright yellow flowers.

SITE: Bright light, but no direct sun. Wrinkled or curled leaves indicate that the plant is getting too much light.

TEMPERATURE: Warm room temperature (65–80°F/18–27°C) all year round.

WATERING: Keep the potting mix evenly moist all year round. Dry potting mix will cause the leaves to wilt or drop off.

FEEDING: Feed monthly in spring and summer with a balanced liquid fertilizer diluted to half strength.

TIP: Wipe the leaves regularly with a damp cloth to keep them glossy and dust-free.

Asparagus densiflorus
Sprengeri Group

(Asparagus fern)

This is not a true fern, but a member of the lily family.

SITE: Bright light, but avoid direct sunlight because it may scorch the foliage.

TEMPERATURE: Average room temperature (60–75°F/16–24°C).

WATERING: Water thoroughly, allowing the potting mix to dry out a little between waterings. Water sparingly in winter, but do not allow the potting mix to dry out completely.

FEEDING: Apply a liquid fertilizer in summer. There is no need for a great amount of care for this plant.

TIP: Keep your asparagus fern where it will get filtered light.

Calathea species

Although fairly common as houseplants, calatheas are still a stunning genus of plants. With bold leaf markings, as well as the bonus of purple undersides to the leaves, they are a great choice for a shady room.

SITE: Light shade in summer. Brighter conditions are ideal in winter, but keep out of direct sun because this can dull the color of the leaves and damage the plant.

TEMPERATURE: Keep warm (at a minimum temperature of 60°F/16°C).

WATERING: Keep well watered in the summer, making sure that the potting mix is kept moist. *Calathea* also enjoys high levels of humidity and so will need regular misting. Brown tips on the leaves indicate that the humidity is too low.

FEEDING: Feed with a very weak solution (half the recommended strength) when watering.

TIP: Do not repot too often, and use a peat-substitute-based potting mix.

**KEEP GOING,
KEEP GROWING**

"Plants want to grow; they are on your side as long as you are reasonably sensible."

—Anne Wareham

Dracaena sanderiana
(Lucky bamboo)

A striking plant with a slender, upright stem and graceful, arching green leaves. This indoor plant is very easy to care for. It can be grown in a vase of water with a few pebbles to keep it upright.

SITE: Bright light, but no direct sun, which will scorch the leaves.

TEMPERATURE: Average room temperature (60–75°F/16–24°C).

WATERING: Change the water every week or two.

FEEDING: Feed every two months with an all-purpose liquid fertilizer. Just a drop will do.

TIP: This plant is sensitive to chlorine, fluoride, and other chemicals often found in tap water. Use distilled or bottled water only.

Exacum affine
(Persian violet)

This is a beautiful flowering houseplant.

SITE: Bright light. Some direct morning sun is fine, but keep out of hot afternoon sunlight, which may scorch the plant.

TEMPERATURE: Average room temperature (65–75°F/18–24°C). Keep the plant away from drafts.

WATERING: Keep the potting mix evenly moist, but do not allow it to become soggy.

FEEDING: Feed fortnightly while the plant is blooming with a balanced liquid fertilizer diluted to half strength.

TIP: Pick off faded flowers to extend the flowering period.

Ficus binnendijkii

This fig is ideal for a bright position. Long, tapered leaves adorn this lush, robust variety. It makes a pleasing alternative to *Ficus benjamina* (weeping fig).

SITE: Bright, indirect light to bright shade. Will tolerate a small amount of direct sun.

TEMPERATURE: Average room temperature (65–75°F/18–24°C).

WATERING: Water regularly in the growing season, but leave to dry out slightly first. Water only rarely over winter. Benefits from an occasional misting.

FEEDING: Apply a liquid feed every month or so.

TIP: Prune to shape in winter if required.

Hedera helix

(Ivy)

These lush, trailing vines have decorative, lobed leaves.

SITE: Bright light, but not direct sun. If a variegated variety of ivy changes to mostly green, then it isn't receiving enough light.

TEMPERATURE: Tolerates a wide range of temperatures.

WATERING: Keep the potting mix evenly moist, but not soggy, from spring through fall (autumn), and slightly drier in winter.

FEEDING: Feed monthly from spring through fall with a high-nitrogen liquid fertilizer.

TIP: If you want to keep your ivy plant within bounds, light pruning can be done at any time of the year.

"Watching something grow is good for morale. It helps us believe in life."

—Myron Kaufmann

CACTUS MAKES

PERFECT

Nephrolepsis exaltata

(Boston fern)

The Boston fern acts as a natural humidifier, absorbing common air pollutants and releasing water vapor.

SITE: Moderate to bright light. No direct sun. Give the plant a quarter turn every week or so to expose all sides to the light.

TEMPERATURE: Average room temperature (60–75°F / 16–24°C).

WATERING: Keep the potting mix constantly moist, but not soggy. Watch large ferns and hanging-basket ferns because they can dry out quickly.

FEEDING: Feed fortnightly all year round with a balanced liquid fertilizer diluted to half strength.

TIP: Fronds that are yellow and wilted are a sign of over-watering. Reduce the amount of water and trim off damaged fronds.

Peperomia species

This compact plant has short stems covered with heart-shaped, deeply ridged leaves. The leaves are green, sometimes with a blush of red, and have dark green veins.

SITE: Low to bright light. No direct sun.

TEMPERATURE: Average room temperature (65–75°F/18–24°C).

WATERING: Keep only barely moist at all times.

FEEDING: Feed monthly from spring through fall (autumn) with a balanced liquid fertilizer diluted to half strength.

TIP: Leaf drop may be caused by a build-up of salts in the potting mix from soft water or too much fertilizer.

Polyscias fruticosa
(Ming aralia)

Interior designers love the ming aralia because it resembles a Japanese maple. The key to caring for this beautiful little tree is moisture and warmth.

SITE: Aim for bright light, although this plant will tolerate varying light levels, from low light to full sun.

TEMPERATURE: Average to warm room temperature (65–85°F/18–29°C).

WATERING: Water thoroughly and allow the potting mix to dry out between waterings.

FEEDING: Feed monthly from spring through fall (autumn) with a balanced liquid fertilizer.

TIP: Cut back on water in the winter when growth has slowed.

Sansevieria trifasciata var. *laurentii*

(Variegated snake plant)

Snake plants are perfect for the modern interior. Boasting long, sword-like leaves with an elegant gold trim, they can reach 3ft (1m) in height and provide strong structure if placed in a group.

SITE: Will tolerate a range of conditions, from full sun to light shade.

TEMPERATURE: Average room temperature (65–75°F/18–24°C).

WATERING: Water when the potting mix is dry, and less over winter. No need for high humidity.

FEEDING: Apply a liquid feed every month or two.

TIP: When the roots of your *Sansevieria trifasciata* have completely filled the pot, it is time for the plant to be divided and replanted.

Saxifraga stolonifera

(Strawberry saxifrage)

This plant grows in a mound of rounded, scalloped leaves with decorative silvery veins. The leaves are hairy with burgundy-red undersides.

SITE: Prefers bright light all year round. Some direct morning sun is fine, but protect from strong sun, which can cause the leaves to fade.

TEMPERATURE: Increase levels of humidity in warmer conditions (anything from 50–75°F/10–24°C).

WATERING: Water thoroughly and allow the top inch or so of potting mix to dry out between waterings. Water less frequently in winter when growth is slower.

FEEDING: Feed monthly in spring and summer with a balanced liquid fertilizer diluted to half strength.

TIP: Dry potting mix can cause dry leaves. Aim to keep the potting mix lightly moist.

"Plants are like people:
they're all different and a
little bit strange."

—John Kehoe

BOTANY PLANTS

LATELY?

Spathiphyllum species
(Peace lily)

This flowering houseplant from South America is very easy to care for. It responds to average indoor conditions better than many houseplants.

SITE: Tolerates lightly shaded areas.

TEMPERATURE: Average room temperature (65–75°F/18–24°C).

WATERING: Keep the potting mix evenly moist. Use a pot with a good drainage hole to prevent soggy potting mix, which can cause root rot.

FEEDING: Feed monthly in spring and summer with a balanced liquid fertilizer diluted to half strength.

TIP: This plant is poisonous. Keep it away from children and pets who may play with or chew on parts of the plant. Wash your hands thoroughly after handling it.

Tradescantia "Isis"

(Spider lily)

These plants can be either trailing or tufted perennials,
usually with fleshy, evergreen foliage and distinctive
three-petaled flowers.

SITE: Place in partial shade.

TEMPERATURE: Average to warm room temperature
(65–80°F/18–27°C).

WATERING: Water thoroughly, and then allow the top inch
or so of potting mix to dry out between waterings.

FEEDING: Feed monthly in spring and summer with a
balanced liquid fertilizer diluted to half strength.

TIP: Pot on to a larger pot in spring.

Yucca species

These are very tolerant architectural plants.

SITE: Bright light to full sun.

TEMPERATURE: Cool to average room temperature (50–75°F/10–24°C).

WATERING: Keep the potting mix moist in spring through fall (autumn). In winter, water just enough to prevent the potting mix from drying out.

FEEDING: Feed fortnightly with a balanced liquid fertilizer in spring and summer.

TIP: You can put yuccas outside for summer where they will get some direct sun each day. Outdoors, they may produce tall spikes of fragrant white flowers.

Yucca elephantipes
(Spineless yucca)

Like other members of the *Yucca* family, the spineless variety will tolerate full sun.

SITE: Thrives in a bright position and will tolerate direct sun. Although yuccas tolerate some shade, spin the plant around from time to time or the branches will lean toward the light.

TEMPERATURE: Being fairly hardy, it will thrive in most situations. WATERING: Keep well watered in summer, but water infrequently in winter. The more you water over the summer, the faster the plant will grow. It's advisable to let the plant dry out before watering again.

FEEDING: Apply a liquid feed every three weeks or so over summer (less if you want to restrict growth).

TIPS: Use a free-draining potting mix. The plant can be put outside over the summer months.

Zamioculcas zamiifolia

(ZZ plant)

Each of the branches growing from the potting mix is, in fact, a leaf and the "leaves" are leaflets growing out of them. An easy plant for almost every room.

SITE: Prefers light shade, although it will tolerate some sun as well.

TEMPERATURE: Average room temperature, but not below 65°F (18°C) in winter.

WATERING: Allow the surface of the potting mix to dry out before re-watering. Water sparingly over winter.

FEEDING: Apply a very weak liquid feed every month or so over the growing season.

TIPS: The ZZ plant can be divided and replanted when repotting is required. Do not let the plant get too wet, as rotting can occur over the winter if it is over-watered.

Creating your indoor oasis

Choosing and grouping containers

When choosing a container for your houseplant, the most important consideration is to ensure that your plant and pot are in proportion. Your choice will inevitably be influenced by personal preference, but you should also take the time to check that the container will work aesthetically where you are going to position it.

Your new houseplant will probably come in a plastic pot, unless you are buying one that has already been planted up in its "smart" container. This is when you can choose a container that reflects your personal style and surroundings, bearing in mind that a fussy and highly patterned pot may detract from the impact of the plant. It is very important to check that the container has holes at the bottom so that water can drain away and so prevent the plant from rotting.

Also, if you are grouping plants together, make sure the containers match and preferably group them together in odd numbers to enhance the aesthetics of the arrangement.

Terrariums

Terrariums are great for growing indoor plants in today's centrally heated and air-conditioned homes. Growing plants in a closed glass case, or terrarium, means that water evaporating from the leaves during transpiration condenses on the glass and then trickles down the sides of the case to be reabsorbed by the roots.

Unlike their Victorian predecessors, terrariums today are both affordable and suitable for smaller homes. They are a wonderful way to keep succulents and cacti indoors, preventing them from rotting or drying out. They also make a great project for the whole family.

You'll need to decide whether you would like your terrarium to be open or closed. Open terrariums can tolerate some direct sunlight, but be aware that too much sun may burn any leaves that are in direct contact with the sides of the terrarium. In contrast, closed terrariums need a location where they will receive bright light, but no direct sunlight. If they are placed in direct sunlight, the temperature inside the terrarium can rise considerably and "cook" the plants. (A closed terrarium may also be an open terrarium that has a cover.)

Whether you opt for an open or closed terrarium should also be determined by your choice of plants—sun-loving plants yearn for natural light, so use an open terrarium, while plants that require high levels of humidity need a closed terrarium. Mind-your-own-business (*Soleirolia soleirolii*), violas, mosses, and cacti and succulents will all grow well in any type of terrarium.

Glass vases

It is unusual to grow plants in potting mix in a glass container, as their roots don't fare well when exposed to the light. However, they make great receptacles for creating water gardens and growing aquatic plants. Adding some pebbles will help to reduce the light levels.

Clay containers

Containers made from clay or terracotta can prove both practical and versatile when you're growing houseplants. You can choose terracotta pots in their natural color or paint them to blend in with your décor or environment. Because terracotta is a porous material, the pots will lose water from their sides, as well as from the base, so may need watering more frequently. Using a decorative mulch or topping (see page 33) can help to reduce excess evaporation.

Wooden crates

A wooden crate makes a great partner for lush foliage plants and can be kept natural or painted to match your environment. Wood is not watertight, however, so you will also need to give the crate a plastic lining. Be careful when watering, because you don't want the plants' roots to become waterlogged. Alternatively, you can make a few holes in the base of the crate to allow excess water to escape, but take care that draining water doesn't cause any damage to the surface the crate sits on.

Hanging objects

Even if space is at a premium, you can still introduce interesting foliage into your home by using hanging objects as containers. They can also make a striking focal point in a room.

Window boxes

A window box is a great way to use space on your window ledges, both inside and out. Choose boxes that complement your space.

Handmade objects

You will derive a great deal of pride and pleasure from making your own containers, whether you are just reusing household items or making them from scratch. I have used a variety of handmade objects in the book, so look through the projects to see if you feel there are any you would enjoy making yourself.

China and porcelain containers

These are available in a vast array of shapes and sizes, as well as lots of different colors and designs. When designing a container grouping, I usually make sure that the containers complement one another in all these areas. Using lots of different patterns, colors, and textures not only makes a display look messy, but can also distract your attention from the plants. Ceramic containers are unlikely to have drainage holes, so make sure you remove any excess water after watering.

Metal containers and wire crates

Containers made from metal are wonderfully contemporary and also a great way to recycle unusual objects. Few have drainage holes, but you can easily make these yourself using a drill or a hammer and nail.

Raise a glass

These three differently shaped wine glasses are perfect for bringing added interest to the display on the previous page. Here, I used a mix of different succulents, as well as some bun moss, to create a little world of interest. You can place a few pebbles in the base of the glasses to provide extra drainage, but as long as you remember that these plants don't require lots of water, they should be fine. I have not included any potting mix here, but the succulents should last as long as the moss is kept moist.

Color contrast

Neon colors are startling and fresh in the modern home. An instant hit of color automatically lifts any interior—and is perfect for a white-toned home. I chose two solid, round zinc planters and carefully painted a neon-red strip around the top with paint bought at my local craft store. I then chose two green succulents (*Aeonium* "Dinner Plate" and *Crassula*) and planted them in the center of the pots. It's a simple look that adds an injection of color.

I love the simplicity of this project. Using plants with different forms, but with the same color tone, will allow them to shine. One of the most interesting features of this display, along with the unusual textures and shapes, is the juxtaposition between the fresh green of the plants and the vibrant red of the pots. This color combination is an aesthetic treat for the eyes.

French flair

Walking through the streets of Paris and looking up to the sky, you will often see apartments lined with window boxes and lushly planted balconies. Parisians love to grow their own herbs and produce to use in cooking, and don't see a lack of outdoor space as a hindrance.

You can often find wooden crates in vintage and antiques stores. I picked up this one at an antiques market and particularly liked the markings of the Mondot Saint-Émilion wine—a good vintage, I've been told! The rustic-looking crate is now a picturesque miniature French herb garden planted with thyme, rosemary, and lavender.

Thyme is easy to grow indoors; it simply needs a bright windowsill and some basic care and attention to thrive. The heady scent emanating from rosemary is delicious, and this highly fragrant herb can be used in many dishes. Being a Mediterranean herb, it will appreciate a sunny spot. Finally, the lavender plant makes a lovely partner for both the thyme and the rosemary. Lavender is hard to resist, boasting beautiful flowers and an equally arresting scent. It gives a delicate flavor to cooking and is especially wonderful in light desserts.

Up in the air

Traditional hanging baskets can seem staid and fussy, with too many plants crowded into a small space. This beautiful metallic container breaks the rule, however, as it's both handsome and simple—great for a stylish bedroom or perhaps displayed at the top of a flight of stairs. The delicate, glossy leaves of *Pellaea rotundifolia* (button fern) tumble over the edge of the container, making for an easy, uncluttered look. A small, low-growing fern, it is easy to grow and creates a unique look with its small, rounded leaflets.

Set in stones

This handsome trio of glass terrariums (opposite and overleaf) features an eclectic selection of cacti, stones, and green mosses in open glass vases.

Attractive vases are easy to get from homeware stores, but it's a good idea to shop around to find vases that you particularly like and which will work in your indoor space. Think about where you want to put them, how much space you have, and how much light the space receives.

The three vases pictured here are all different shapes and sizes, but still work well as a single display. Inside each one is a selection of pebbles that I collected from walks on the beach. Try to choose pebbles and pretty shells with different colors and textures that will contrast well. Pretty shells can also look striking in glass displays. I also found some pieces of granite and dried moss, which I used in the display to create different pockets of interest.

In the cylindrical vase, I used floristry sheet moss, which is lined with paper, making it easier to cut and shape to fit inside containers. This lush green moss creates a great juxtaposition with the desert-like appearance of the other vases. The fossils and small Lithops (living stones or stone plants) are a nod to archeological discovery. Finally, I added a beautiful green gemstone to represent a pond surrounded by glistening rocks.

Spa sanctuary

Bathrooms are all too often neglected spaces for indoor plants. It's a great shame to see a single plant sitting by itself in the corner, or even no greenery at all! However, bathrooms make wonderful backdrops for indoor plants, as they are often flooded with light—these bright spaces allow plants to shine.

The succulents and bright, fleshy plants in this wonderfully dark arrangement all thrive in the warm surroundings of a bathroom. These plants also all retain moisture well and boast a beautiful depth of color.

On the table is a tall *Maranta leuconeura* (prayer plant), with its stunning combination of colors that are set off by the dark clay pot. The patterns and coloring of this plant's leaves easily make it one of the most attractive plants in any arrangement. Its leaves partially fold up at night, just like hands at prayer.

You should be careful for whom you buy the plant below and on the left, which is known as mother-in-law's tongue. It is more diplomatic to call it by its botanical name—*Sansevieria trifasciata*. This is a dense, succulent perennial with stiff, sharp, evergreen leaves.

The dark green *Aloe haworthioides* on the right is a really luxuriant plant with its spiky, fleshy leaves. It is a great plant for a bathroom and easily grows in full sun to partial shade. It flowers in late summer and early fall (autumn) and has beautifully delicate apricot blooms with a deliciously sweet fragrance.

Why does
my plant
do that?

Plants often react in the same way to adverse conditions, such as pest and disease attacks, a lack of light, or over- and underwatering—with yellow or browning leaves or wilting stems, or by shedding their leaves. Try to work out what the problem may be by asking yourself a few questions: Are you watering correctly? Are you feeding correctly? Does the plant have enough light? Is the pot the right size? The following guide may help you to identify the cause of the problem.

Wilting

POSSIBLE CAUSE: Underwatering can have a dramatic effect on a plant, which seems to wilt overnight. Since the potting mix will probably be coming away from the sides of the container, it's difficult for the plant to absorb any water.

SOLUTION: Check the potting mix regularly to see if it is dry, and water if necessary. To revive it, move it to a cool area, out of direct sunlight, and submerge the container in a bowl of tepid water. Leave to soak for about half an hour and then let the container drain for 10 minutes. (You can weigh the container down with a large pebble if it starts to float up.) The plant should show signs of recovery in about an hour. Soaking the plant in this way will lead to a good rate of transpiration and kick-start the plant into reviving itself.

Yellowing leaves

POSSIBLE CAUSE: Underwatering. When plants are too dry, they cannot take up water, which also contains valuable nutrients.

SOLUTION: Check the potting mix regularly to see if it is dry, and water if necessary.

•

POSSIBLE CAUSE: Overwatering. Waterlogged roots cannot function and thus are unable to provide the plant with water and nutrients.

SOLUTION: Make sure the pot has ample drainage holes and also that it's not standing in a water-filled saucer.

•

POSSIBLE CAUSE: Lack of nutrients. Nitrogen is essential to the production of a green pigment called chlorophyll, which harnesses light energy so that the plant can photosynthesize. If a plant is short of nitrogen, the available nitrogen moves to the top of the plant where it's most needed, resulting in the bottom leaves turning yellow.

SOLUTION: Regular feeding.

POSSIBLE CAUSE: Low temperatures. Yellowing leaves may occur if a plant is used to warm temperatures.

SOLUTION: Move the plant to a warmer position.

•

POSSIBLE CAUSE: Hard water, which raises the lime content, on lime-hating plants.

SOLUTION: Use soft water or a feed that is specific to neutralize the lime.

Leaf, flower, or bud drop

POSSIBLE CAUSE: Underwatering. The plant sheds leaves
or flowers to conserve moisture.

SOLUTION: Check the potting mix regularly to see if it is dry,
and water if necessary.

•

POSSIBLE CAUSE: Changes in light levels. Leaves can
become detached as they adjust to the new light levels.

SOLUTION: Avoid turning the plant dramatically too often.

•

POSSIBLE CAUSE: Changes in temperature,
which can shock the plant.

SOLUTION: Provide stable growing conditions.

Scorched leaves

POSSIBLE CAUSE: Not enough moisture. Leaves lose water faster through transpiration than it can travel up the plant from the roots, so the leaves turn brown at the edges.

SOLUTION: Move the plant to a more humid area.

•

POSSIBLE CAUSE: Too much heat. Hot conditions such as those found near radiators or from direct sunlight may scorch the plant.

SOLUTION: Move plant to a cooler area.

Pests

Aphids (greenfly)

WHAT TO LOOK FOR: Distorted stems and leaves; damaged flowers; sticky honeydew on plants.

SOLUTION: Rub the insects off by hand or use a biological nematode control.

•

Leaf rolling caterpillars

WHAT TO LOOK FOR: Nibbled leaves and stems; rolled-up leaves with a fine, sticky webbing holding them together; distorted growth caused by leaves or shoots that are stuck together.

SOLUTION: Pick off the caterpillars with your fingers or use a biological nematode control.

Mealy bug

WHAT TO LOOK FOR: Yellowing leaves; tufts of waxy white wool in leaf axils; honeydew on leaves.

SOLUTION: Dig out the bugs or use a biological nematode control.

•

Red spider mite

WHAT TO LOOK FOR: Mottled or finely spotted leaves; curled-up leaf edges; a fine, silky webbing on leaves and on the underside of leaf axils.

SOLUTION: Use a biological or chemical nematode control.

•

Soft scale insects

WHAT TO LOOK FOR: Sticky substance on leaves, which may turn black; waxy brown or yellow encrustations on the underside of the leaves.

SOLUTION: Rub the insects off with your fingers or use a biological nematode control.

Vine weevil (Larva)

WHAT TO LOOK FOR: Wilting of the whole plant, even when the potting mixture is moist; roots or tubers eaten away.

SOLUTION: Use a chemical or biological nematode control.

•

Vine weevil (Adult)

WHAT TO LOOK FOR: Crescent-shaped sections eaten out of leaves.

SOLUTION: Pick off the weevils with your fingers or use a chemical control.

•

Whitefly

WHAT TO LOOK FOR: Sticky honeydew on plants; pure white insects on the underside of leaves.

SOLUTION: Use a biological nematode control.

Diseases

Blackleg

WHAT TO LOOK FOR: Strikes where the stem meets the potting mix (normally when the mix is kept too moist). Leaves turn yellow and the stem turns brown up to 4in (10cm) above the soil.

SOLUTION: Always make sure the potting mix can drain properly by providing adequate drainage holes. You may have to dispose of the plant completely, however, and start again by taking cuttings, as the parent plant will probably not recover. Take the cuttings from the top of the plant and dip the ends in hormone rooting power containing a fungicide before potting up.

•

Botrytis (Gray mould)

WHAT TO LOOK FOR: Fluffy gray mold on half-rotted leaves.

SOLUTION: Spray with a fungicide.

Crown or stem rot

WHAT TO LOOK FOR: Soft, slimy stems; black
and brown decayed areas.

SOLUTION: Take cuttings from unaffected areas, and spray
with sulphur before repotting. Unfortunately, this rot may be
fatal to the parent plant.

•

Fallen petal mold

WHAT TO LOOK FOR: Fallen petals left on
leaves can rot and cause mold.

SOLUTION: Remove damaged leaves.

•

Powdery mildew

WHAT TO LOOK FOR: Powdery white patches on leaves.

SOLUTION: Pick off affected leaves and spray
the plant with a fungicide.

Sooty mold

WHAT TO LOOK FOR: Thick, black, soot-like deposits on
leaves and stems, growing on honeydew produced by
sap-sucking insects.

SOLUTION: Wash the leaves regularly with a soapy liquid
such as diluted dishwashing liquid.

Index

Picture credits

Front cover © Adobe Stock/bonezboyz
Back cover above © Adobe Stock/MaryDesy
Back cover below © Adobe Stock/bonezboyz

1 © Adobe Stock/MaryDesy; 2 Ph Rachel Whiting/Styled by Selina Lake; 3 Adobe Stock/MaryDesy; 5 © Adobe Stock/bonezboyz; 7 Adobe Stock/tanya; 12 Ph Rachel Whiting/Paul West @consideredthings; 15 Adobe Stock/gigirosado; 18 Ph Rachel Whiting/the home of Marie Emilsson www.trip2garden.se; 24–25 Ph Rachel Whiting/ the Fresh Flower Company workshop in East Dulwich www.freshflower.co.uk; 26 Adobe Stock/bonezboyz; 31 © Adobe Stock/gigirosado; 32 Ph Rachel Whiting/an artist's house in the Netherlands; 34–35 Ph Rachel Whiting/ Susanna and David le Mesurier's home in Wales; 36 © Adobe Stock/MaryDesy; 42 Ph Rachel Whiting/Styled by Selina Lake; 44–45 © Adobe Stock/jchizhe; 51 Ph Rachel Whiting/the Fresh Flower Company workshop in East Dulwich www.freshflower.co.uk; 59 © Adobe Stock/andwill; 60 © Adobe Stock/NtDanai; 62 © Adobe Stock/bonezboyz; 64 © Adobe Stock/twilight mist; 67 © Adobe Stock/elenarostunova; 68 © Adobe Stock/Michail; 71 © Adobe Stock/Creative by Nature; 73 © Adobe Stock/MaryDesy; 75 © Adobe Stock/ Thosapon; 76 © Adobe Stock/wichatsurin; 79 © Adobe Stock/Yurii; 80 © Adobe Stock/Matthias de Boeck; 82 © Adobe Stock/gigirosado; 84 © Adobe Stock/ berna_namoglu; 87 © Adobe Stock/SASITHORN; 88 © Adobe Stock/Kginger; 91 © Adobe Stock/Roni; 92 © Adobe Stock/coulanges;94 © Adobe Stock/MaryDesy; 96 © Adobe Stock/Vladimir Liverts; 99 © Adobe Stock/dropStock; 100 © Adobe Stock/ LKovoleva; 103 © Adobe Stock/gilles lougassi; 104 © Adobe Stock/kseniaso; 106 Ph Rachel Whiting/the Fresh Flower Company workshop in East Dulwich www.freshflower. co.uk; 109 Ph Rachel Whiting/the home and shop of Katarina von Wowern of www. minaideer.se; 111 © Adobe Stock/nurofina; 112 © Adobe Stock/nurofina; 128 Ph Benjamin Edwards/the home of Kay Prestney @kinship_creativedc; 130 © Adobe Stock/gigirosado; 133 © Adobe Stock/Creative Juice; 135 © Adobe Stock/Creative Juice; 141 © Adobe Stock/Creative Juice; 142 Ph Rachel Whiting/the home and shop of Katarina von Wowern of www.minaideer.se.